SO WHAT IS TOLERANCE ANYWAY?

JOHN LAMACHIA

the rosen publishing group / rosen central

new york

Published in 2000 by The Rosen Publishing Group, Inc.
29 East 21st Street, New York, NY 10010

First Edition

LaMachia, John
        So what is tolerance anyway? / by John LaMachia.
            p. cm. — (A student's guide to American civics)
        Includes bibliographical references and index.
        Summary: Examines the importance of practicing tolerance for others,
        the causes and effects of prejudice and discrimination, and the
        problems that may occur when people are intolerant.
            ISBN 0-8239-3099-8
            1. Toleration—United States Juvenile literature. 2. Prejudices—
        United States Juvenile literature. 3. Discrimination— United States
        Juvenile literature. 4. United States—Ethnic relations Juvenile
        literature. 5. United States—Race relations Juvenile literature.
        [1. Toleration. 2. Prejudices. 3. Discrimination.]
        I. Title.   II. Series.
        HM1271.L35 1999
        305.8' 00973—dc21   99–32769
                                                                        CIP

Manufactured in the United States of America

so what is tolerance anyway?

CONTENTS

INTRODUCTION
WORKING TOGETHER FOR DEMOCRACY

The founding fathers of the United States—Thomas Jefferson, George Washington, and John Adams—were responsible for creating a new kind of government. By writing the Declaration of Independence, the U.S. Constitution and the Bill of Rights, these and other leaders established the United States as a democracy. In a democracy, every citizen is entitled to certain rights and freedoms, such as the right to choose the leaders of their country. The rights of American citizens are guaranteed by the Bill of Rights, the first ten amendments to the U.S. Constitution. A constitution is a document that defines the powers of the government of a country and the basic rights of its citizens.

The U.S. Constitution guarantees that all American citizens are protected equally under the law. While the Constitution can enforce fair treatment, it cannot force people to think in a fair or tolerant manner. As a citizen in a democracy, you are responsible for helping to promote tolerance. It is your duty to help create an environment in which people's differences are accepted, respected, and appreciated. In this book, we will discuss what tolerance means, how tolerance is an essential part of democracy, and what happens when people are intolerant of one another.

America's founding fathers, Jefferson (top), Washington (middle), and Adams (bottom) created a democratic U.S. government

so what is tolerance anyway?

TOLERANCE AND MINORITY RIGHTS

The word "tolerance" means a willingness to listen and learn from people who are different from you in some way. That difference might be skin color, religion, sex, age, ethnicity, culture, or physical ability. The United States was founded on the idea of tolerance. That is because a democracy only works when everyone has a chance to voice his or her opinion. In a democracy, the majority rules. That means that the opinions shared by the largest number of people often have the most influence. The majority, however, is not always right.

The U.S. Constitution promises that intolerance will not be allowed to keep the minority (those not in the majority) silent. The Constitution has an obligation to make sure that all people, including those in the minority, have an opportunity to voice an opinion and be heard. In many cases, tolerance and fairness have required that laws be created that go against the wishes of the majority. These laws come in the form of amendments, or changes to, the U.S. Constitution. Here are two examples of constitutional amendments that were added to guarantee the rights of those in the minority.

Learning about different cultures can help you to be a tolerant person.

THE ABOLITION OF SLAVERY

Starting in the 1600s, thousands of Africans were brought to America against their will to work as slaves. Slaves were thought of and treated as property, like a house or a crop of wheat. They were bought and sold by "masters," and often members of slave families were sold off separately from one another. Slaves worked long, grueling hours for no pay. Many slaves received little food and few clothes and were often whipped or beaten. Slaves were not allowed to vote or to receive an education. According to the

Slaves were often abused by their masters.

U.S. Constitution, slaves were "three-fifths of all other Persons." This meant that slaves were not considered by the majority of the U.S. population to be whole human beings. The treatment of slaves was based on the views of the majority of white Americans at that time.

By the eighteenth century, there were many people, black and white, who thought that slavery was wrong. People who fought for the abolition, or end, of slavery were called abolitionists. Most abolitionists lived in the North, where slavery had been outlawed in the mid-1800s. Many abolitionists, such as Frederick Douglass, Harriet Tubman, and Sojourner Truth, were former slaves. Although they were in the minority, the abolitionists voiced their opinions loud and clear. They spoke for the black people—a minority group that, because of the conditions of slavery, often wasn't able to speak for itself. The abolitionists held marches, gave speeches, and wrote letters and articles calling for the end of slavery.

In 1861 the Civil War began in the United States, in part over the issue of slavery. The northern states went to war against the southern states. The North won, and in 1865, the Thirteenth Amendment made slavery illegal. All former slaves became citizens of the United States. They were not, however, granted all the rights that other citizens

Frederick Douglass (top), Harriet Tubman (middle), and Sojourner Truth (bottom) were three of America's most famous abolitionists.

enjoyed. Black men were not given the right to vote until the Fifteenth Amendment was passed in 1870. And black women, along with white women, would have to wait fifty more years to be granted that right.

THE RIGHT TO VOTE

Until 1920, the Constitution did not grant women the right to vote. Because men were the majority in the U.S. Congress—in fact, the government was made up entirely of white males—women and their interests were not represented. Not only were women denied the right to vote, but in many states women were not allowed to own property, sign contracts, hold government office, practice law or medicine, or serve on a jury.

During the mid- and late-1800s and early 1900s, thousands of women used their First Amendment right of free speech to protest the unfair law that kept them from voting. People who fight for the right to vote are called suffragists. Suffragists strongly believed that women, as citizens of the United States, had the right to have a say in who represented them. Susan B. Anthony, Elizabeth Cady Stanton, and Carrie Chapman Catt were three leaders of the women's suffrage movement. They and other suffragists organized protests, pressured Congress, and even risked arrest and jail in support of their cause. Over time, they gained popular support for this right. Finally, in 1920, the minority—in this case, women—convinced the majority that the law was unfair and needed to be changed. The Nineteenth Amendment was passed, giving all women the right to vote.

Like people, nations can only grow through change. And like people, nations never change unless they start to see things in a new way. The authors of the Constitution knew that the United States needed laws to make sure that intolerance didn't deny certain citizens their rights. These laws forced people to provide basic freedoms to every citizen, and to listen to the minority. Being open to minority opinions allows the majority to see things differently. Tolerance allows people, and nations, to change and grow.

Women voting and handing in their ballots at a polling station for the first time.

| so what is tolerance anyway?

Melting Pot or Land of Diversity?

The United States is made up of many different kinds of people. The first people of North America were Native Americans. Then in the early 1600s, Europeans began to settle in America. Not long after, Africans were brought to America as slaves. By the late 1700s, the black population in the United States had grown quite large. In the early 1800s, a wave of people immigrated to the United States from Germany, England, Ireland, and Scandinavia. At the beginning of the 1900s, another wave of immigrants arrived, mainly from southern and eastern Europe. In the 1960s, more groups of immigrants began to arrive, mostly from Asia and Latin America. According to the United States Immigration and Naturalization Service, this trend continues. Immigrants arrive in large numbers from Mexico, the Philippines, Vietnam, China, and the Dominican Republic. These groups have changed the make-up of America dramatically. Today, the population of the United States is about 270 million—83.4 percent white (including Latino), 12.4 percent black, 3.3 percent Asian, and 1 percent Native American.

In the past, people often referred to the United States as a melting pot, a place where immigrants blended into the established American culture. Blending in was necessary to be accepted and to be successful.

People of many different ethnicities live in America.

CHAPTER TWO

KWANZAA

One example of a holiday that honors a specific culture is Kwanzaa. While Kwanzaa itself is not an African festival, many of its elements are taken from African traditions. Kwanzaa is considered an African-American celebration of life. Dr. Maulana Karenga, a Nigerian, created this festival in the United States in 1966. It was meant as a celebration of the first harvests. The first harvests in many African countries happen during their summer season, which is December and January.

Dr. Maulana Karenga, founder of Kwaanza

On December 31, family members gather for a feast. Many of the dishes that are served are traditional African harvest foods. Many families wear special clothes that resemble styles of traditional African dress.

Today, rather than trying to become more alike, many immigrants celebrate the ways they're different from other Americans. Immigrants teach their children to speak their native languages. Families follow and pass on native customs and traditions. Immigrants want to keep aspects of their original culture and ethnicity alive. They also want to preserve their heritage.

There are people whose families have been in the United States for many generations, and who may be unfamiliar with their heritage. Some young people have decided to find out more about their families' culture and traditions. Some learn the languages their parents or grandparents spoke in the "old country." Many learn to cook traditional foods and wear elements of traditional clothing. Others choose to celebrate holidays that honor a particular people or culture.

The Chinese Lion Dance takes place at many Chinese New Year festivals.

so what is tolerance anyway?

Living in a nation with so many different kinds of people gives you a unique opportunity to learn about other cultures. You can try foods from all over the world, including Thai, Ethiopian, and Indian. You can wear clothes that are inspired by different cultures, like Scandinavian clogs and Irish fishermen's sweaters. You can buy CDs featuring Latin rhythms, Caribbean Reggae, or traditional Japanese music. You may eat Passover dinner with your Jewish friend and celebrate the breaking of the Ramadan fast with your Muslim classmate. You can celebrate Cinco de Mayo with your Mexican American classmate and Chinese New Year with your Chinese American friend. All you need to do to take advantage of these opportunities is to have an open mind and be tolerant of people who are different from you.

During Ramadan, Muslims study the Koran and then break the fast with a special meal.

so what is tolerance anyway?

Culture or Stereotype?

CHAPTER THREE

The first step in learning tolerance is to understand and appreciate differences among people of different cultures. A culture is a set of rules, expectations, and beliefs that a group of people live by. A person's culture influences his or her appearance, language, values, traditions, customs, food, clothing, and music. A culture also may be based around a religion. In many Middle Eastern countries, much of the culture centers on the Muslim faith. For many Jewish people, religion dictates the foods they eat, the clothes they wear, and the way they associate with people outside the Jewish faith. Understanding your own culture, and respecting the cultures of others, helps a person to become more tolerant of people's differences.

When you don't know very much about another culture, you may think everyone from that culture is the same. We pick up ideas about different cultural groups from our own experiences, stories or jokes we've heard, or from movies and television. We may assume these ideas are true for all people of that culture. These kinds of ideas are called stereotypes.

A Muslim woman prays at Al Aqsa Mosque in Jerusalem during Ramadan.

STEREOTYPES

Stereotypes are unreliable generalizations that are based on false information. They result from variations among groups of people, including differences in age, gender, skin color, physical ability, or economic backgrounds. Stereotypes are applied to all members of a group without taking into account individual differences.

Stereotypes are used to categorize people. Some people apply stereotypes when they meet someone who is different from them. They may feel afraid or threatened by a culture they don't know or understand. Applying stereotypes may give the user a sense of control. If someone uses stereotypes, he or she loses the chance to get to know people from different cultures as individuals. Instead, the stereotyper simply lumps those people together with everything they know about their culture as a whole—true or untrue.

PREJUDICE

The word "prejudice" means having a negative view about a group of people before you know all the facts. Like stereotypes, prejudice stems from judging a person based on the characteristics of a group to which he or she belongs. The group could be a specific religion, culture, race, sexual orientation, or ethnicity.

Prejudice is a result of prejudging someone based on stereotypes rather than on facts or personal knowledge. When a person is prejudiced, he or she exaggerates the negative stereotypes about a group of people. Someone who is prejudiced may repeat stereotypes, such as, "Latino people are lazy," "Blondes are dumb," "Jewish people are cheap," "Teenagers are delinquents." People who are prejudiced

Obviously not all blondes are dumb, since this blonde actress, Kellie Martin, attended Yale University.

may promote stereotypes by telling jokes or insulting a particular group of people. They also may act in hostile ways toward those who are unlike them. Prejudice is an extreme form of intolerance.

DISCRIMINATION

The term "discrimination" refers to the prejudicial treatment of individuals or a group of people based on their differences. There are many examples of discrimination in the history of the United States. Women were once discriminated against by not being allowed to vote, own property, or keep any money they earned. In the early 1900s, European immigrants, including Germans, Poles, and Italians, were discriminated against because they could not speak

English. Black people were discriminated against—and often still are—because of their skin color.

Stereotypes, prejudice, and discrimination are major forms of intolerance. They happen because people do not understand the history, values, customs, and beliefs of cultures that are different from their own. This lack of understanding leads to judging people according to one's own standards, which may or may not apply.

Prejudice and discrimination are destructive. They break down a society. A democracy cannot work well when the people who live in it think and act with prejudice and intolerance. When tolerance is not practiced, it can lead to serious consequences, including suspicion, hatred, harassment, assault, and even murder.

Discrimination against blacks in America included the creation of separate drinking fountains (left) and movie entrances (below).

INTOLERANCE IN HISTORY

Perhaps the most extreme example of intolerance in recent history is the Nazi treatment of the Jewish people during World War II. Adolph Hitler, the leader of Germany's Nazi party, believed that Aryans, or people of northern European descent, were the "master race." He thought that all other people, particularly Jewish people, should be eliminated. He managed to convince millions of other people that he was right. The result was that six million Jewish people, along with gypsies, gays, and the physically disabled, were starved, tortured, and murdered. Unfortunately, there are many more instances of extreme intolerance throughout history—in America and all over the world.

THE CONFLICT OVER KOSOVO

Since 1998 the ethnic Albanians (people who were born in another country but are Albanian by heritage) have been killed or forced to leave their native land of Kosovo. Kosovo is a province of the country of Serbia. Ethnic Albanians make up the majority of the population of Kosovo. They would like Kosovo to become a country independent of Serbia. The Serbs, however, consider Kosovo an important part of their history and

Jewish inmates of the Warsaw ghetto smuggling in supplies, winter 1940

their country. They would rather kill or push the ethnic Albanians out of the country than lose control of Kosovo. The Serbs have killed thousands of ethnic Albanians, and forced more than half a million others to flee their native land. This effort is called "ethnic cleansing." The Serbs are trying to "clean" their country of ethnic Albanians, and in so doing, destroy an entire culture.

Many Serbs see ethnic Albanians as terrorists or rebels. They believe that the ethnic Albanians are wrong in defying the Serbian government and trying to gain independence for Kosovo. Many Serbs do not view ethnic cleansing as an extreme form of intolerance; rather, they see it as a way to preserve their own culture.

DISCRIMINATION AGAINST JAPANESE AMERICANS

On December 7, 1941, Japanese forces bombed Pearl Harbor in Hawaii. More than 2,400 Americans were killed. It was the first time that a foreign war touched U.S. soil, and it was the event that pushed the United States to enter World War II.

A great wave of fear swept across the United States following the attack

American battleships burning after the Japanese attack on Pearl Harbor

on Pearl Harbor. At the time, there were approximately 125,000 people of Japanese descent living throughout the United States, including 70,000 Japanese Americans who were U.S. citizens by birth. Much of the general public suspected that anyone of Japanese descent might have loyalties to Japan that were stronger than those to the United States. Many people thought that Japanese Americans were secretly working for the Japanese government and meant to harm the United States. In response to these fears, the government rounded up 112,000 Japanese Americans who were living on the West Coast. They were forced to leave their homes, businesses, and jobs behind and relocate to internment camps. Internment camps were areas where people were confined based solely on their

Japanese Americans waiting in line for food in an internment camp

ethnicity. Japanese Americans were kept in government internment camps from 1942 to 1945.

There were eleven World War II Japanese internment camps scattered throughout the western states. The camps had small, cramped buildings, often with dirt floors and crowded sleeping conditions. There, the Japanese Americans were treated like criminals, though they were never proven disloyal to the United States.

Finally, at the end of the war in 1945, the Japanese Americans were released and allowed to return to their homes. However, many had lost their homes and savings, and had little to return to. Intolerance on the part of the American people and the U.S. government shattered the lives of hundreds of thousands of innocent Japanese Americans.

In 1988 the U.S. Congress passed the Civil Liberties Act, which offered $20,000 and a letter of apology to each person who had been imprisoned. Former President George Bush wrote a letter

Former President George Bush

saying, "We can never fully right the wrongs of the past, but we can take a clear stand for justice and recognize that serious injustices were done to Japanese Americans during World War II."

DISCRIMINATION AGAINST ARABS

On February 26, 1993, a bomb went off in an underground parking garage in the World Trade Center in New York City. The World Trade Center is made up of two of the largest buildings in the world. More than 100,000 people work in and visit the buildings every day. The bomb killed six people and injured more

Police escort injured workers from the World Trade Center following the blast that killed six people.

than one thousand others. It left a crater that was 1,000 feet square and three stories deep. Six Arab Muslim men, Ramzi Ahmed Yousef, Mohammad Salameh, Nidal Ayyad, Mahmud Abouhalima, Ahmad Mohammad Ajaj, and Abdul Rahman Yasin, were suspected of having planted the bomb. Five of them were tried and found guilty.

In the months following the World Trade Center bombing, many Americans were afraid of Arabs, Arab Americans, and Muslims. News broadcasts sometimes referred to Arabs or Muslims as terrorists. Arabs who applied for U.S. citizenship felt that their applications were delayed because they were being examined more closely than other people's applications. Many Arab Americans felt that they were being harassed by the police and airport customs officials. The entire Arabic community was unfairly judged based on the actions of a few people.

DISCRIMINATION AGAINST GAYS AND LESBIANS

A person who is gay, or homosexual, is attracted to members of the same sex. Many people are uncomfortable with the idea of two men or two women loving each other. They have a low tolerance for any kind of love that is different from what they know or feel. Some people turn this discomfort into violence. According to the National Coalition of Anti-Violence Programs, the number of attacks against gays and lesbians dropped from 2,665 in 1997 to 2,552 in 1998. The attacks themselves, however, have become more brutal.

One example of such violence was the murder of Matthew Shepard, who died on October 12, 1998. Shepard was a twenty-one-year-old gay college student at the University of Wyoming. Russell Henderson and

Aaron McKinney pistol-whipped Shepard, and left him tied to a fence in freezing October weather for eighteen hours. Shepard died as a result of this treatment. Henderson was sentenced to two consecutive life terms in prison. As of spring 1999, McKinney had yet to go to trial.

This and other acts of intolerance encouraged President Clinton to expand federal hate crime laws to include violent acts based on the sexual orientation of the victim. Clinton supports programs that help educate middle school students about intolerance. One such youth program is run by the Anti-Defamation League, an organization that helps educate people about the dangers of intolerance and evils of prejudice.

HIV AND AIDS DISCRIMINATION

Since the first appearance of the HIV virus, which is believed to cause AIDS, there has been fear and suspicion about people who are infected with the virus. Although many people still believe that only gay men contract HIV and AIDS, this is incorrect. Heterosexual (straight) men, as well as women, teenagers, and children, can also get HIV and AIDS. One example of a teenager who was infected with AIDS was Ryan White. Ryan contracted the disease while receiving a blood transfusion in 1984. He was thirteen years old when he learned that he only had a short time to live. He decided that he wanted to return to school and continue his life like any normal teenager.

Ryan's school in Kokomo, Indiana, however, was not so sure of his right to do so. The school board, the teachers, and even the principal voted to keep Ryan out of the school. Rumors spread, and soon people believed they could catch AIDS from Ryan if they shook hands with him or shared a pencil. Despite the fact that AIDS can only be transmitted through bodily fluids, such as blood and saliva, people in the community were frightened.

Ryan went to court to fight for his right to attend school. Nine months later he won that right, but he still had to face extreme prejudice. At school, Ryan was forced to use a separate bathroom and drinking fountain, and he wasn't allowed to participate in gym class. Classmates spread lies accusing Ryan of biting people and spitting on cafeteria food. He became the target of cruel jokes, and his locker and schoolbooks were regularly vandalized. People in the community avoided Ryan, even going so far as to get up and move if he sat down near them.

Ryan's situation in Kokomo was widely publicized. Famous athletes, musicians, and actors showed their support for Ryan. Ryan testified before the President's Commission on AIDS and campaigned for AIDS education in schools. At age eighteen, Ryan died from the disease. In his honor, the Ryan White Foundation was established. The foundation educates students about HIV and AIDS and fights for tolerance toward people living with these illnesses.

Ryan White

BLACK AND WHITE

The United States has a long, terrible history of intolerance against African Americans. Beginning with slavery, many black people have been made to feel as though they are less valued in society than are white people. There are some blacks who consider whites to be racists. Sadly, there are still many instances of intolerance between the two groups. When this kind of extreme racial hatred surfaces, incidents like the murder of James Byrd, Jr. occur.

On June 7, 1998, a black man named James Byrd, Jr., was walking on the side of a road in Jasper, Texas. Three white men, John William King, Shawn Berry, and Lawrence Brewer, picked up Byrd in Berry's

The Byrd family in the courtroom during John William King's trial

truck. They took Byrd to a wooded area, beat him, chained him to the back of the truck by his ankles, and drove for nearly three miles on a bumpy road. Byrd died from the injuries he suffered. The three men did this just because Byrd was black. King was given the death penalty for his role in the crime. As of spring 1999, Berry and Brewer had yet to go to trial.

Intolerance in any form is unacceptable. But these types of violent acts resulting from intolerance are unbearable. The only way to keep this kind of violence from occurring is to teach tolerance and confront and oppose intolerance when we encounter it.

John William King after being sentenced to death. He is wearing a bulletproof vest to prevent being shot by assassins.

so what is tolerance anyway?

PATHWAYS TO TOLERANCE

Although no two persons are exactly alike, people are more alike than they are different. We all need to eat, sleep, and breathe. Most people live in communities made up of families, friends, and neighbors. If you realize how much we all have in common, it can be easier to see past any differences.

Unfortunately, there are some people who are too afraid to give up their stereotypes and judgments. They fear people who are different from themselves. They don't know how to interact with them. Often they resort to insults, jokes, and hateful remarks instead. They hold on to their prejudices and discriminate based on those opinions. Fear and intolerance can grow and spread, becoming a dangerous threat to individuals, cultures, and entire nations. Here are some things you can do in your own community to combat intolerance.

HAVE AN OPEN MIND

You might hear a lot about someone before you meet him or her. You might find out what country that person is from, what he or she looks like, how he or she dresses. It is possible to judge somebody based on this

People are more alike than they are different.

information, before you have even met the person. Often people let their prejudice, intolerance, and fear form their opinion of someone. Without having given this person a chance, they have already decided how they feel about him or her. If you have an open mind, if you avoid prejudging someone, it won't matter what other people say. A person with an open mind accepts people for who they are, not for what he or she has heard about them.

EDUCATE YOURSELF

You may hear things about a person, a certain group of people, a religion, a country, or even an illness without having any idea if those things are true. This misinformation could lead someone to think or act intolerantly. An example of this kind of prejudicial thinking surrounds the HIV virus, which is believed to cause AIDS. Many people are so afraid of getting HIV and AIDS that they say and believe things that are simply untrue, such as ways that the virus can be transmitted. For example, you might think you can catch HIV just from touching someone who has the virus, or touching something that person has handled. These ideas are false. If you take the time to educate yourself about HIV, or whatever else you are hearing about, you can make smart decisions for yourself about what to believe. Once you are informed, you will be able to think and act in an appropriate way toward a person or situation.

TREAT PEOPLE AS INDIVIDUALS

Each person is a little different from another: skinny or heavy, black or white, short or tall, Hindu or Catholic, quiet or loud, gay or straight. Differences alone cannot tell you what that person is like. You may know

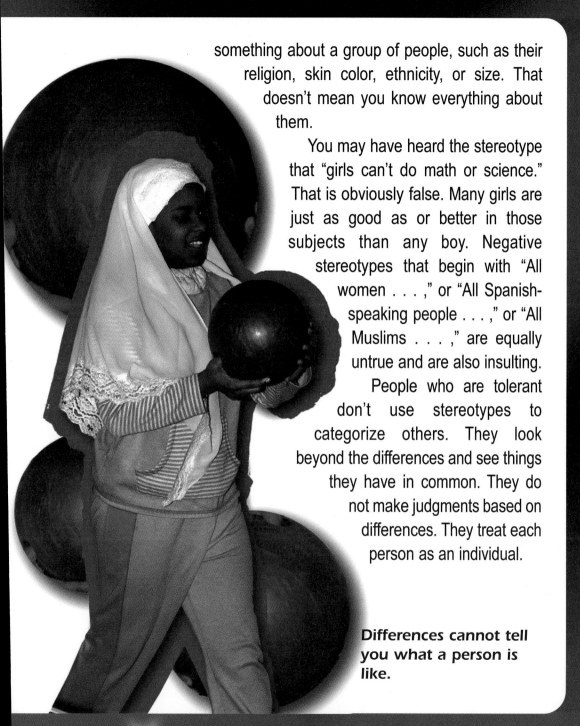

something about a group of people, such as their religion, skin color, ethnicity, or size. That doesn't mean you know everything about them.

You may have heard the stereotype that "girls can't do math or science." That is obviously false. Many girls are just as good as or better in those subjects than any boy. Negative stereotypes that begin with "All women . . . ," or "All Spanish-speaking people . . . ," or "All Muslims . . . ," are equally untrue and are also insulting.

People who are tolerant don't use stereotypes to categorize others. They look beyond the differences and see things they have in common. They do not make judgments based on differences. They treat each person as an individual.

Differences cannot tell you what a person is like.

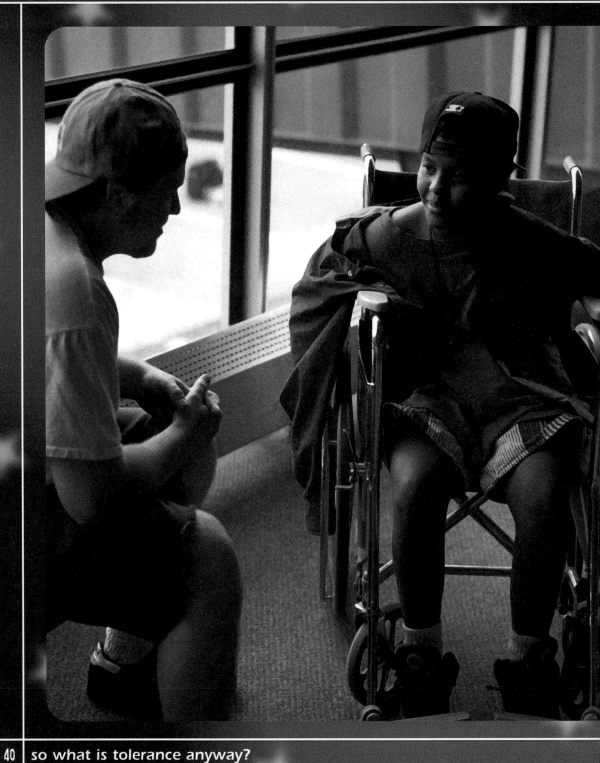

so what is tolerance anyway?

PRACTICE AND TEACH TOLERANCE

One way to teach others tolerance is to be tolerant yourself. If you treat people with respect and kindness, and take the time to understand and communicate with them, those around you may do the same.

Another way to promote tolerance is by refusing to approve of or excuse intolerant behavior. If you find yourself in a situation where offensive stereotypes or hateful language are being used, take a stand for what's right. It may be hard to confront someone who is acting intolerantly, but it is also important that you let that person know how you feel. Explain to the speaker why you thought his or her remark was offensive. Show support toward the person who was insulted. Convince others to follow your example.

Sometimes all it takes is one person to start a trend of tolerance. You can be that person by showing tolerance toward those who are different from you and promoting tolerance in your community. You can start by thinking about what it means to be tolerant. This definition is from the United Nations' "Declaration of Principles on Tolerance": "[Tolerance is] respect, acceptance and appreciation of the rich diversity of our world's cultures, our forms of expression and way of being human. It is fostered by knowledge, openness, communication and freedom of thought, conscience and belief. Tolerance is harmony in difference."

Getting to know people despite their differences is one way to fight intolerance.

GLOSSARY

abolitionist A person who actively opposes slavery.

AIDS acquired immune deficiency syndrome; a severe disease spread by contact with body fluids such as blood and saliva.

amendment A change to something.

bill of rights A document that lists and protects the individual rights of people.

citizen A person who by birth or choice is a member of a nation.

civil rights The nonpolitical rights of every citizen, no matter what his or her race, color, religion, or sex.

constitution A document stating the powers of a country's government.

culture The beliefs, customs, art, religions, and traditions of a group of people.

democracy A government that is run by the people who live under it.

descendent A person born of a certain family or group.

discrimination The act of treating a person badly or unfairly just because he or she is different.

ethnic cleansing The act of removing an entire group of people sharing the same language, origin, or culture.

ethnicity Background based on race, religion, nationality, or culture.

heritage The cultural traditions that are handed down from parent to child.

HIV human immunodeficiency virus; the virus that may cause AIDS, spread through body fluids.

immigrant A person who moves to a new country from another country.

internment camp An area where people are confined based on their ethnic background.

majority The group of people that is the largest and has the most power or say in a population.

minority A group of people that is in some way different from the larger part of a population.

prejudice Hatred of a group of people just for being a member of a different culture, race, or religion.

protest A statement or act in which a person or group objects strongly to something.

responsibility A sense of duty or the obligation to take care of something or someone.

sexual orientation The preference a person has for someone of a particular gender.

slavery The system of one person "owning" another.

stereotype The belief that everyone in a group shares the same characteristics.

suffragist A person who fights for the right to vote.

terrorist Someone who commits violent acts to scare a population or a government.

tolerance Acceptance of differences among those with different customs, values, lifestyles, or looks.

FOR FURTHER READING

Duvall, Lynn. *Respecting Our Differences*: A Guide to Getting Along in a Changing World. Minneapolis: Free Spirit Publications, 1994.

Citykids. *Citykids Speak on Prejudice*. New York: Random House, 1994.

Scott, Sharon. *Not Better, Not Worse, Just Different*. Amherst, MA: Human Resource Development Press, 1994.

Gillam, Scott. *Discrimination: Prejudice in Action*. Springfield, NJ: Enslow, 1995.

Phillips, Angela. *Discrimination*. New Discovery, 1993.

Garg, Samidha. *Racism*. Austin, TX: Raintree/Steck-Vaughn, 1997.

Senna, Carl. *The Black Press and the Struggle for Civil Rights*. Danbury, CT: Franklin Watts, 1993.

Haughton, Emma. *Equality of the Sexes*. Danbury, CT: Franklin Watts, 1997.

Fremon, David K. *Japanese-American Internment in American History*. Springfield, NJ: Enslow, 1996.

Hamanaka, Sheila. *The Journey: Japanese Americans, Racism, and Renewal*. New York: Orchard Books, 1990.

Lowis, Peter. *South Africa*. Austin, TX: Raintree/Steck-Vaughn, 1995.

RESOURCES

Museum of Tolerance
9786 West Pico Boulevard
Los Angeles, CA 90035
(310) 772-2505
Web site: http://www.wiesenthal.com/mot/index.html

The Foundation for Religious Tolerance
Web site: http://www.religioustolerance.net/

Citizens Committee for New York City
e-mail: info@citizensnyc.org
Web site: http://www.citizensnyc.org/

Anti-Defamation League
823 United Nations Plaza
New York, NY 10017
(212) 885-7800
(212) 490-0187 (fax)
Web site: http://www.adl.org/

Arab American Anti-Discrimination Committee
Web site: http://www.adc.org/index.html

INDEX

ABOUT THE AUTHOR

John LaMachia is a freelance writer with an avid interest in U.S. history and government. He lives in Upstate New York.

PHOTO CREDITS

Cover photo, p. 6 by Thaddeus Harden; pp. 5, 8, 9, 11, 22, 27, 29, 33 © CORBIS/Bettman; p. 5 © CORBIS/Museum of the City of New York; p. 9 © Archive Photos; pp. 12, 36, 39, 40 © Skjold; p. 14 © Hakim Mutlaq; p. 15 © CORBIS/Karen Su; p. 16 © CORBIS/Michael Boys; pp. 16, 18, 34, 35 © CORBIS/AFP; p. 21 © CORBIS/William Norton; p. 24 © CORBIS/Archives of Mechanical Documentation, Courtesy of USHMM Photo Archives; p. 28 © CORBIS/Seattle Post-Intelligence Collection; p. 30 © Archive/Reuters/Mark Cardwell/Archive Photos.

Design and Layout
Kim M. Sonsky

Consulting Editors
Mark Beyer and Jennifer Ceaser